Traveling Through Grief

Tammy Dahlgren

BookLeaf Publishing

India | USA | UK

Presentation by *BookLeaf Publishing*

Web: www.bookleafpub.com

E-mail: info@bookleafpub.com

ISBN: 9789360948054

First edition 2024

Big Momma

Excited for time to be
Just Ma Mae and me
Traveling together to Mississippi
Not knowing the sadness I'd find
Because of loved ones left behind
We had to go to bury the dead
Because of neighborly love we were well fed
Big Momma was Ma Mae's mother
The teacher and the nurturer
Giving love to her family like no other
Death did not care that I was five
I witnessed shared grief and wanted to hide
I did not know loss could bring so much pain
And your family would be forever changed.

Ma Mae

Here we go again death came knocking
Except this time I was not the one traveling
We had to wait for family and friends
Before we could let the healing begin
This time I was ten
It was as if I'd lost my best friend
Although it was thirty six of us grands
I always felt I was the only one
Out time together was very dear
Her love for me I will forever hold near
She taught me to show love towards all
And to help them up when they fall.
That to me was an important lesson
Having her shape my life was the greatest
blessing.

Mr. Nutter

At seventeen, I was tasked with caring for the
elderly
Making sure their needs were met
And their dignity remained in tact
A patient, Mr. Nutter would be one I would
never forget.
He was in his eighties around my Papa's age
He was dying as I sat by his side
Making him comfortable until he died
I watched him take his last breath in peace
Helped to establish my humanity
Little did I know at the time
In a few weeks it would help me keep my sanity
Mr. Nutter's passing helped me to understand
The dead cannot cause me any harm
So much calm and comfort washed over me.
In a few weeks I was prepared to accept that
death was knocking at my door
Like it had before.
This time it was my papa.

Papa

When Ma Mae died
We showered Papa with love in abundance
Summer vacations were always fun as we
traveled across the Midwest
Visiting places like St Louis and Detroit
Taking him to see his relatives
We traveled until he became ill
That was the day that our world stood still
When he passed my graduation was a few weeks
away.
Had he been alive he would have been there
Always showing us support and loving care.

Honeymoon and Divorce

I was married a few years after high school.
I wanted to share with my husband things I had
done in my youth.
We honeymooned in Wisconsin Dells
We later discovered I was pregnant
I lost my baby in the first trimester.
We lost two more babies and because of the
stress and grief
We decided to divorce
He planned a trip to Germany
A trip I would have loved to take
I had never been overseas
Needless to say he went alone
While I stayed in the house before striking out
on my own.

Milwaukee

After a failed marriage, it was time to move to
another state
Milwaukee,Wisconsin was do be my new home
I had relatives there so I wouldn't really be alone
It was close enough to home that in an
emergency
I could arrive home quickly
And for just the cost of a tank of gas
Once I settled in things went smoothly
I secured a job, a car, a man and later a child.

Michael

Michael was a cousin I loved like a brother
He had sickle cell anemia and was a favorite of
my mother.
He aspired to find the cure for his disease.
That dream was not realized
The disease won
He lost his life when he was young
My grief was hard
My grief was long
I did not know how I was going to move on
A few months later
I enlisted my sisters in a drive to NYC
To show the children the Macy's day parade
It was an experience we hadn't had
When we arrived the parade was done
We still made sure the children had fun
We went to FAO Schwarz and the top of the
Empire State Building
When we arrived back home
I faced the reality that Michael was gone.
He has lived on in my heart.

Russia

I had become a travel agent.
My father was excited about my career change.
You girls should travel he would always say.
Now, I was on my way.
I was blessed with the opportunity to travel to
Russia
I had booked my trip and my father called to let
me know he was scheduled for hip replacement
surgery
It was a week before I was to travel to Russia.
I wanted to support my family
I wanted to go on this trip
My dad said for me to go it will be all right
A week before my trip they canceled the
surgery.
My dad told me to go and enjoy.
I went to the Hemitage Museum, the Bolshoi
Theater, and the Moscow Circus
What an adventure.
When I returned home my dad had his surgery.
He went to recovery and suffered complications.
He passed away two days later.

Chicago

My son and I traveled two hours to the hospital
in Chicago to see my dad before his surgery.
I got to share my trip and give gifts to the
family.
They came in and prepared him for his surgery.
We hugged and kissed and told him we would
see him soon.
The surgery went well and off to recovery he
went.
They transferred him to a room.
We went to see him and hugged and kissed
again.
Shortly afterwards the complications begin.
He struggled with breathing.
They rushed him to the ICU
They stabilized him.
My mom sent us home
We drove back to Milwaukee at her command.
We called the next morning and all was well.
We went about our daily life.
When I arrived home we had missed several
calls from my mom telling us to come back to
the hospital.
We drove the two hours back to Chicago.
It was March.

Generally a cold day in the Midwest.
This day the weather was exceptionally warm
and the sun was shining brightly.
We arrived at the hospital and my mom us when
we got off the elevator.
My dad had passed before we arrived.
We left the hospital and went to Gary, Indiana.

Gary, Indiana

We gathered at our family home.
Now arranging my father's funeral.
It was hard to be at home without my father
there.
We decided to have him cremated.
It was decided because it was too hard to have a
viewing of the body.
We had changed the family custom to cremation
for all going who died from that day forward.

Spring Break

Before my father passed , my sister and I had
planned a trip to Savannah, Georgia, Myrtle
Beach, South Carolina and Charleston, South
Carolina.
Since my father passed away.
My sister decided she did not want to go.
We canceled the trip.
Spring break was spent in Gary with my family.
We did take a trip to Myrtle beach as a family
three years later.
I traveled to Charleston with a friend.
Years later I met friends in Savannah.

Atlanta

My son and I moved to Atlanta once he
graduated high school.
My sister had moved to Atlanta five years prior.
My niece and son were like best friends.
He wanted to be close to her.
With nothing keeping me in Milwaukee, we
moved.
Once we were settled in, my niece became ill.
She had a brain tumor and one and a half years
later she passed away.

Africa

I longed to go to Africa.
Because of roots, I wanted to go to Senegal.
Later I decided to go to Ghana.
They were celebrating their emancipation from th UK.
This was perfect for me as I was celebrating my own emancipation.
When I arrived in Ghana I made my way to Elmina Castle to see the door of no return.
After my tour of the castle, I sat on the beach looking towards the ocean.
I said a prayer for all the women in my family who had passed away. Big Momma, Ma Mae, Aunt Bessie, Aunt Jeanette and now my niece, Reanie.
This trip was for them as well as for me.
It was a trip to honor their memory.

Acapulco

A year after my dad died, I wanted to treat my
mom to a trip to Acapulco.
Neither of us had been there. I wanted her to
relax.
It was a trip just for the two of us.
She missed her husband so much.
I knew I could not bring him back.
I wanted to share a new adventure with her.
When she arrived back home
She told her friends where she had gone.
She became the authority of all things Acapulco.
Where to eat , where to see the cliff divers, how
to get around.
They took her advice and planned their trip.
They thank her for her wonderful tips.

Lee Ann

I met and married Jerry.
Jerry was from Portland Oregon.
He received a call that his brother's wife had died.
Off we went to be with his brother in rainy Portland.
My sister-in-law's name was Lee Ann
She was a wife, a stepmother and an Adam Lambert fan.
I was happy to be there for family and lend a hand.
To help lessen the stress an untimely death can bring.
So we listened to Adam Lambert sing.

Atlanta

I went to Chicago to visit my mother
We almost got into an accident. We got into a
discussion. I mentioned that I did not want to die
there. She said I was born there. We chuckled.
A few months later she visited Atlanta.
She entered the hospital a day later. I received a
phone call that she was in the hospital. After
assessing the situation I decided not to go. A
month later, I received another call informing
me, she was in the hospital again. This time I
traveled to Atlanta.
The doctors told her her options.She decided not
to do the procedure. They told her she would
die.
She began saying her goodbyes. She did not
want any funeral or memorial services. She told
me to go home. I did.
Four days later my son called to let me know she
passed.
I believe she went to visit family and once she
got sick decided like me if she was going to die
it wouldn't be in Gary.

Portland

My mom had left me one third of her 401 (k). I was able to bring my three minor granddaughters from Atlanta to Portland for two weeks in the summer. I shared with them all the wonderful places I enjoyed about Portland. We went to the Multnomah Falls,Timberline Lodge, Mount Hood, the Oregon Caves, Crater Lake. I wanted to create experiences and memories for them. We enjoyed some local favorites as well. Salt and Straw Ice Cream and Slappy Cakes.

Pops

Pops was the father I met him later in his life
I was going to be his son's wife.
The father who showed me the true meaning of
love.
When he accepted and embraced me in freedom.
He cherished his son
And wanted him to be happy
He did not care when he discovered
this brown girl his son was to marry
Pops was eighty-eight and proof positive
that change is never too late.
There maybe sacrifices to be made
Like moving to Portland to be by his side
So he could know in your heart he will always
reside.
I loved him as only I could
Because he loved me as if I was his blood.

Covid-19

Covid-19 changed so many things.
The world was shutdown.
People were loosing loved ones in death.
Being with family helps to comfort and heal.
Like so many others, we had family members to
pass away.
My uncle passed away. We could not honor him
in person.
I did a memorial card and sent it to the family.

I will grieve him in Paris

When my niece was recovering , I spoke to her
that if she died we would have to pry her
mother's hands away from her.
If something happened to my son , I would
grieve him in Paris.
Unfortunately, my son died. I looked at my
husband Jerry and said"now I have to go to
Paris.
A few months later Jerry and I were headed to
Paris and Nice.
We would eat at French cafe's, tour the Muse'e
d'Orsay, and see the Eiffel Tower. In Nice would
would take a food tour. We visited Monaco and
Monte Carlo.
I love Jerry for planning this trip.
It was a welcomed distraction. I will always
miss my son no matter where I am.
He will always be with me in my heart!

Grief and Travel

When I think of travel, I think of relaxation and escape.
Traveling through grief becomes a time of reflection.
How am I going to navigate my world without this important person in my life?
I travel because I can't stop being curious.
I want to see all that was created for me.
Even though my people can't be with me physically.
In my heart they will always be.